MW01622813

SHE'S A
Mom
IF YOU THINK
HER HANDS ARE FULL,
YOU SHOULD SEE HER
HEART

As you create a home, don't get distracted with a lot of things that have no meaning for you or your family. Don't dwell on your failures, but think of your successes. Have joy in your home. Have joy in your children. Have joy in your husband. Be grateful for the journey.

—Marjorie Pay Hinckley

Children
are NOT a
distraction
from more
important work.
They are
THE MOST
important work.

—C.S. LEWIS

She broke the bread into two fragments
and gave them to her CHILDREN,
who ate with eagerness.
"She hath kept NONE for herself,"
grumbled the sergeant.
"Because she is not hungry," said a soldier.
"No," said the sergeant,
"because she is a

mother."

—Victor Hugo

MOTHER LOVE
IS THE
FUEL THAT
ENABLES
A NORMAL HUMAN BEING
TO DO THE IMPOSSIBLE.
—MARION C. GARRETTY

YOUTH FADES, LOVE DROOPS, THE LEAVES OF FRIENDSHIP FALL; A MOTHER'S SECRET LOVE OUTLIVES THEM ALL.

—OLIVER WENDELL HOLMES

MOTHERS
HOLD
THEIR CHILDREN'S
HANDS
FOR A WHILE,
BUT THEIR
HEARTS
FOREVER.

Not always
eye to eye,
but always
heart to heart.

The **JOY in MOTHERHOOD** comes in moments. There will be hard times and frustrating times, but amid the challenges there are *shining* MOMENTS OF *joy* and satisfaction.

—M. Russell Ballard

Mother:

{Muh*th*-er} **-noun**

1. One person who does the work of twenty. For free.

(See also: "angel" and "saint.")

mothers
yours is the work of **salvation,**
and therefore you will be
MAGNIFIED,
compensated, made more than you are
and better than you have ever been
as you try to make
an *honest* effort,
however feeble you may
sometimes feel that to be.

—Jeffrey R. Holland

There is no *perfect* way to be a good mother.

Each situation is *unique*. Each mother has different challenges, different *skills & abilities*, & certainly different children....

What matters is that a *mother* loves her children deeply.

—M. Russell Ballard

A MOTHER
IS SHE WHO CAN
take the place of all others,
BUT WHOSE PLACE
NO ONE ELSE
CAN TAKE.

—CARDINAL GASPARD MERMILLOD

Kristen was finishing a **GRADUATE DEGREE** and had recently given birth to her second child. She felt the **OTHER GRADUATES HAD ACCOMPLISHED** so much more and was reluctant to attend the graduation dinner. Her fears were confirmed when, at the dinner, the students were asked to list their professional accomplishments. Kristen recalled: "I suddenly felt **EMBARRASSED AND ASHAMED.** I had nothing to call myself, no lofty position, no impressive job title." To make matters worse, the professor read the lists as he presented a diploma to each student. The woman ahead of Kristen had many **ACCOMPLISHMENTS:** she already had a PhD, was receiving a second master's degree, and she'd even been a mayor! The woman received **GRAND APPLAUSE.**

Then it was Kristen's turn. She handed the professor her blank sheet, trying to hold back the tears. The professor had been one of her teachers and had **PRAISED HER PERFORMANCE.** He looked at her blank paper. Without missing a beat he announced, **"KRISTEN HOLDS THE MOST CRITICAL ROLE IN ALL OF SOCIETY."** He was quiet for a few seconds, then declared in a powerful voice, **"SHE IS THE MOTHER OF HER CHILDREN."** Instead of a few courteous claps, people rose to their feet. There was just one **STANDING OVATION THAT NIGHT; IT WAS FOR THE MOTHER IN THE ROOM.**

Bonnie D. Parkin, "Sweet Moments," *Ensign*, Nov. 2005, 107.

I REMEMBER MY
mother's prayers
and they have
always
followed me.
They have clung to me
ALL MY LIFE.
—Abraham Lincoln

When God wants a *great work* done in
the world or a great wrong righted, He goes
about it in a very unusual way.
He doesn't stir up His earthquakes
or send forth His thunderbolts.
Instead, He has a helpless baby born,
perhaps in a simple home
out of some obscure *mother.*
And then God puts the idea into the
mother's heart.
and she puts it into the baby's mind.
And then God waits.

—E. T. Sullivan

A **MOTHER** is the truest friend we have, when trials heavy and sudden fall upon us; when adversity takes the place of prosperity; when friends desert us; when trouble thickens around us, still will she cling to us, and endeavor by **HER KIND PRECEPTS AND COUNSELS** to dissipate the clouds of darkness, and cause peace to **RETURN TO OUR HEARTS.**

—Washington Irving

THE BEST MEDICINE IN THE WORLD IS A MOTHER'S HUG.

that is unlike any other love
on the face of the earth.

—Marjorie Pay Hinckley

I'M A MOM.
IF YOU THINK
MY HANDS ARE FULL,
YOU SHOULD SEE
MY HEART.

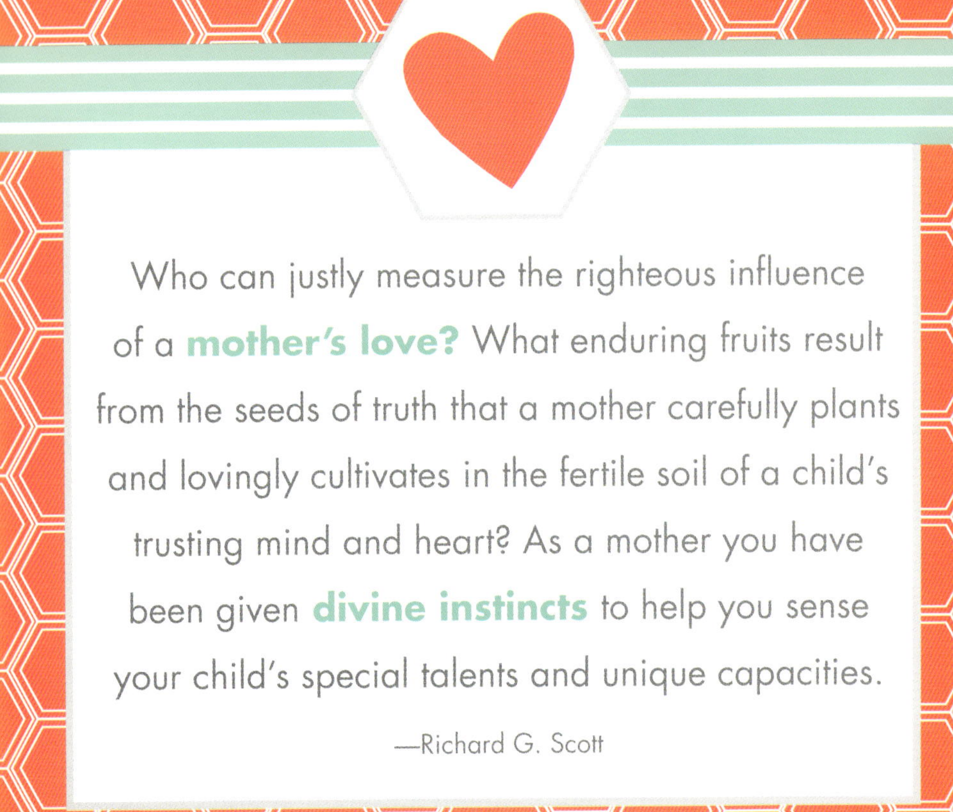

Who can justly measure the righteous influence of a **mother's love?** What enduring fruits result from the seeds of truth that a mother carefully plants and lovingly cultivates in the fertile soil of a child's trusting mind and heart? As a mother you have been given **divine instincts** to help you sense your child's special talents and unique capacities.

—Richard G. Scott

A mother's

HEART

is a special place
where her children are

always

HOME.

The trick is to

enjoy life;

don't wish away your days,

waiting for better ones ahead.

—Marjorie Pay Hinkley

I WILL LET THEM BE LITTLE,
FILL THEIR HEARTS WITH
LAUGHTER,
HELP THEM GROW WINGS,
NURTURE THEIR SENSE OF
WONDER,
INSPIRE THEM TO BELIEVE,
AND LOVE THEM LIKE THERE
IS NO TOMORROW.

THE DAYS ARE

LONG.

BUT

THE YEARS

ARE

SHORT.

—GRETCHEN RUBIN

Sisters, wherever you are, whatever your circumstances may be, you are not forgotten. No matter how dark your days may seem, no matter how insignificant you may feel, no matter how overshadowed you think you may be, your Heavenly Father has not forgotten you. In fact, He loves you with an infinite love.

—Dieter F. Uchtdorf

The following incident occurred in a concentration camp during World War II

One afternoon we had to stand in line to receive our food and water rations. Our mother could BARELY STAND, let alone walk, but she . . . stood in line with us, in obvious pain, leaning heavily on a stick. SEEING MY MOTHER like that fueled the hatred in my heart for those responsible. . . . When I passed one of the officers . . . I threw my cup . . . in his face and spat at him. Immediately a SAMURAI SWORD WAS DRAWN TOWARD ME. Quickly MY MOTHER put her hands on the sword and pushed it away from me, CUTTING HER HANDS. . . .

"Please pick up your cup, Kitty, and apologize," she begged me softly. . . .

With great difficulty she bent and picked up the cup, then bowed deeply. . . . She offered apologies in my name, telling him that I WAS ONLY A CHILD and had not acquired the discipline to master my emotions. . . . "If there must be a punishment," she said, "I WILL TAKE IT FOR MY CHILD."

. . . The officer slowly put the sword back in its sheath, gently took the cup from my mother's hands, and filled it with water. "WOMAN, DRINK!" he said, and . . . my mother drank the water eagerly. He took the cup from her hands, filled it a second time, and offered it to my mother with both hands and a SLIGHT BOW . . .

"IT IS I WHO MUST APOLOGIZE TO YOU FOR NOT RECOGNIZING THE MAJESTY OF YOUR WOMANHOOD," he said.

KITTY DE RUYTER, "A MOTHER'S LOVE," 1998, 19–20.

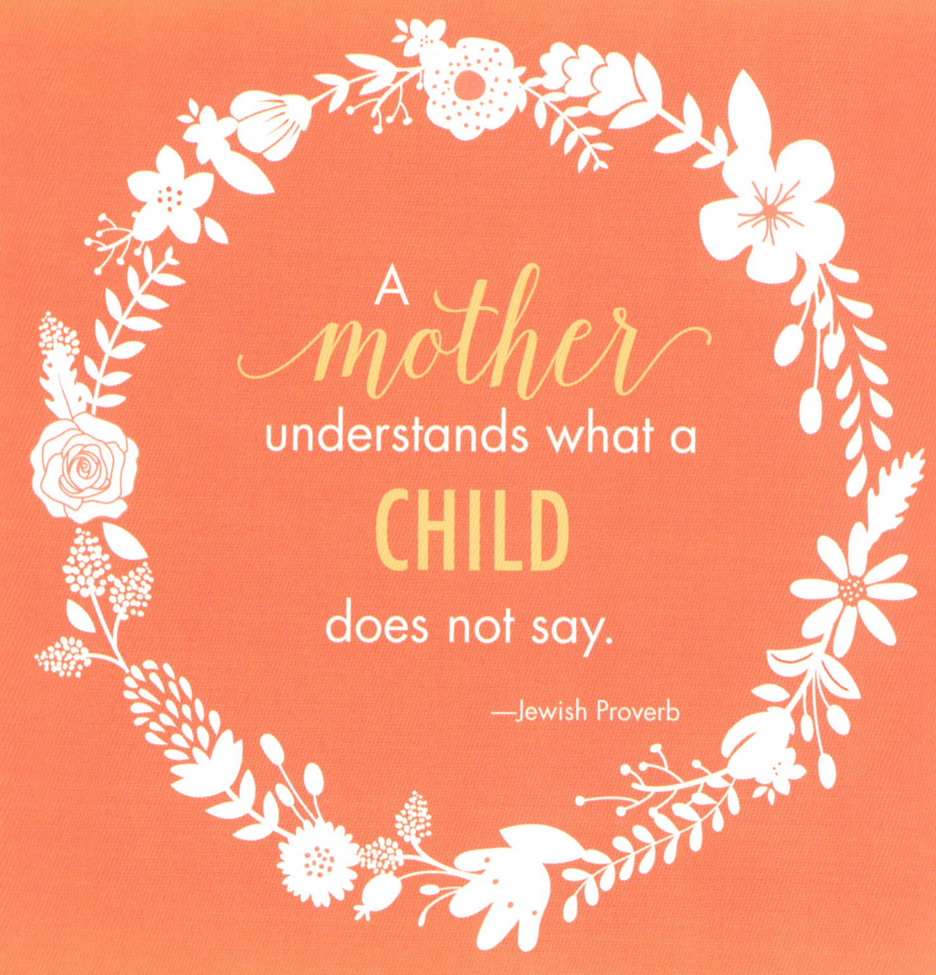
A
mother
understands what a
CHILD
does not say.
—Jewish Proverb

When the real history of mankind is fully disclosed, will it feature the echoes of gunfire or the shaping sound of lullabies? The great armistices made by military men or the peacemaking of women in homes and in neighborhoods? Will what happened in cradles and kitchens prove to be more controlling than what happened in congresses? When the surf of the centuries has made the great pyramids so much sand, **the everlasting family will still be standing, because it is a celestial institution, formed outside telestial time.** The women of God know this.

—Neal A. Maxwell

Motherhood

is near to divinity.
It is the highest,
holiest service to be
assumed by mankind.
It places her who honors its
holy calling and service
next to the ANGELS.

—FIRST PRESIDENCY, THE CHURCH OF
JESUS CHRIST OF LATTER-DAY SAINTS

ALL THAT I AM,
OR HOPE TO BE,
I OWE TO MY
ANGEL
mother.

—ABRAHAM LINCOLN

LIFE

began with waking up and

LOVING

my mother's face.

—George Eliot

You have nothing in this world more **precious than your children.** When you grow old, when your hair turns white and your body grows weary, when you are prone to sit in a rocker and meditate on the things of your life, nothing will be **so important** as the question of how your children have turned out. . . . .Do not trade your **birthright as a mother** for some bauble of passing value. . . . The baby you hold in your arms will grow quickly as the sunrise and the sunset of the rushing days.

—Gordon B. Hinckley

Women bring with them into the world a certain virtue, a *divine gift* that makes them adept at instilling such *qualities as* faith, courage, empathy, and refinement in *relationships* and in cultures.

—D. Todd Christofferson

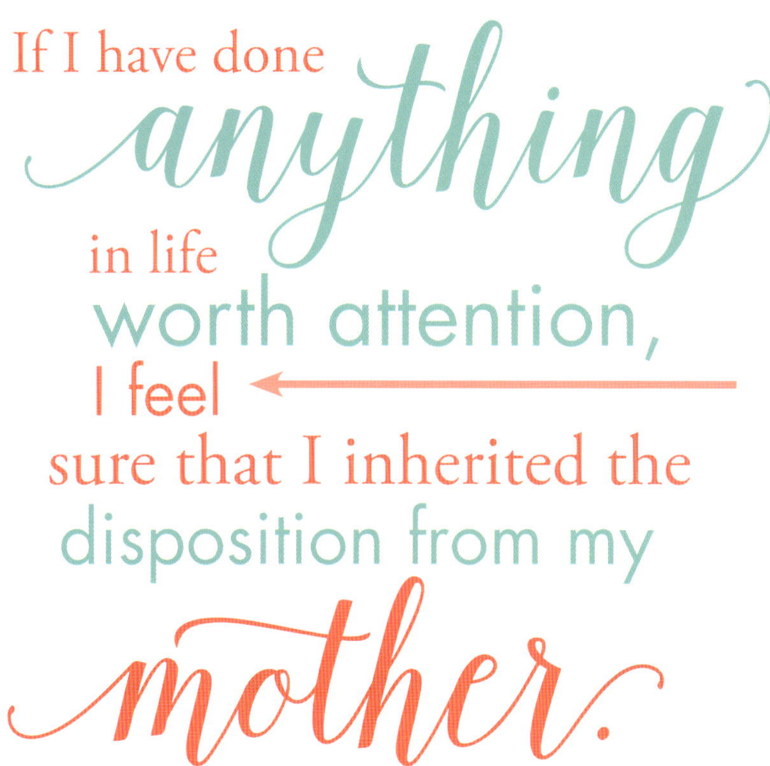

—Booker T. Washington

The *sweetest sounds* to mortals given Are heard in Mother, Home, and Heaven.

—William Goldsmith Brown

Motherhood is a choice you make every day, to put **someone else's happiness** and well-being ahead of your own, to teach the hard lessons, to do the **right thing** even when you're not sure what the right thing is . . . and to forgive yourself, **over and over again,** for doing everything wrong.

—Donna Ball

MY MOTHER GAVE ME LIFE AND NEVER ASKED FOR ANYTHING IN RETURN. THAT IS HER SECRET, YOU KNOW: ALWAYS GIVING WITHOUT EXPECTATIONS. SHE IS AS CONSTANT AS THE SUNRISE, THE MOON, THE STARS AND I COUNT ON HER. SHE HELPS ME FIND MY WAY THROUGH THE YEARS AND MAKES ME LAUGH WHILE DOING IT. THERE ARE SOME THINGS THAT ONLY A MOTHER CAN DO.

—UNKNOWN

THERE ARE
FEW THINGS
more powerful
THAN THE
faithful prayers
OF A RIGHTEOUS
MOTHER.

—BOYD K. PACKER

I plead with you young women to please be more **ACCEPTING OF YOURSELVES,** including your body shape and style, with a little less longing to look like someone else. We are **ALL DIFFERENT.** Some are tall, and some are short. Some are round, and some are thin. And almost everyone at some time or other wants to be something they are not! But as one adviser to teenage girls said: "You can't live your life worrying that the world is staring at you. When you let people's opinions make you self-conscious you give away your power. . . . THE KEY TO FEELING [CONFIDENT] IS TO ALWAYS LISTEN TO YOUR INNER SELF—[THE REAL YOU.]" And in the kingdom of God, the real you is

"MORE PRECIOUS THAN RUBIES."

Jeffrey R. Holland, "To Young Women," *Ensign*, Nov. 2005, 28.

There is no
GREATER GOOD
in all the world than
MOTHERHOOD.
The
influence
of a mother
in the lives of her children
is beyond calculation.
—James E. Faust

My mother was the most beautiful woman I ever saw. All I am I owe to my mother. I attribute my success in life to the moral, intellectual and physical education I received from her.

—George Washington

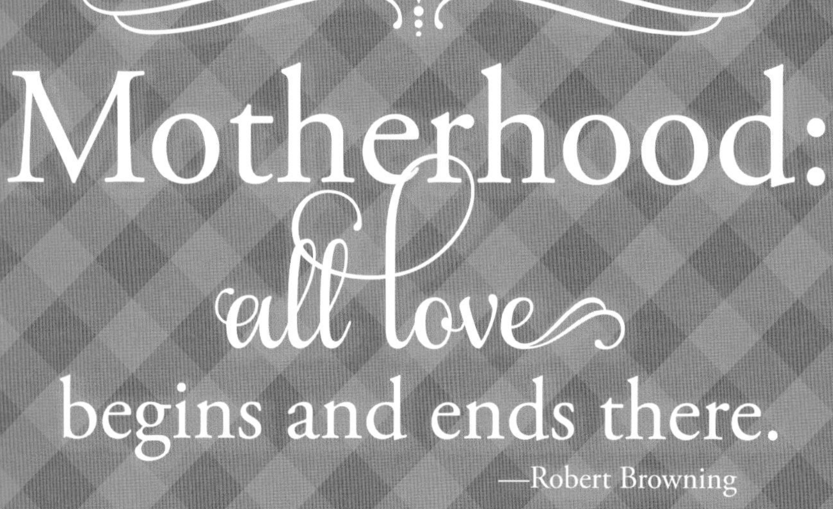
Motherhood:
all love
begins and ends there.
—Robert Browning

If you want to find **greatness,**
don't go to the throne,
go to the cradle.
There is mighty power
in a **mother.** She is the one
who molds **hearts, lives,**
and **shapes character.**

—Flora Amussen Benson

MOTHERS,

YOU ARE DOING

GOD'S WORK.

YOU ARE DOING IT

WONDERFULLY WELL.

HE IS BLESSING YOU &

HE WILL BLESS YOU, EVEN—NO,

WHEN YOUR DAYS

MAY BE THE MOST

CHALLENGING.

JEFFREY R. HOLLAND

MY
greatest
blessings
CALL ME
Mom.

The world has enough women who are tough; we need **women who are tender.** There are enough women who are coarse; we need **women who are kind.** There are enough women who are rude; we need **women who are refined.** We have enough women of fame and fortune; we need more **women of faith.** We have enough greed; we need **more goodness.** We have enough vanity; we need **more virtue.** We have enough popularity; **we need more purity.**

—Margaret D. Nadauld

There is no role
in life more
ESSENTIAL
and more
ETERNAL
than that of
motherhood.

—M. Russell Ballard

Men have to have something
given to them to make them saviors of men,
but not MOTHERS, NOT WOMEN.
[They] are BORN with an inherent right,
an inherent authority,
to be the SAVIORS of human souls . . .
and the regenerating force
in the lives of GOD'S CHILDREN.

—Matthew Cowley

THE *highest and noblest* work in this life is that of a *mother.*

—Russell M. Nelson

DEAR

SISTERS,

MANY OF YOU ARE ENDLESSLY *compassionate and patient* WITH THE WEAKNESSES OF OTHERS.

Please remeber ALSO TO BE COMPASSIONATE AND PATIENT *with yourself.*

—DIETER F. UCHTDORF

IS THE CHOICE
TO BECOME ONE OF THE
greatest SPIRITUAL
TEACHERS THERE IS.

—OPRAH WINFREY

One summer morning,. . . I told my mom I was going out to the playground. She said okay, but told me not to come running back in with muddy feet because she was in the middle of washing and waxing the floor.. . . I must have played for an hour, and at least half of that time was spent in the mud. Then, knowing my mom would probably be finished with the floor and would read to me, I ran home full of boyish excitement and vigor. That same vigor kept me and my mud-covered feet going right up the steps, through the door, and halfway onto the nearly finished wash-and-wax job my mother was still stooped over.

Not waiting for a reaction and not wanting to leave my sin half finished, I ran across the rest of the floor, into my parents' room, and slammed the door shut. Not knowing if I should jump out the second-story window or if just hiding under the bed would do, I burst into tears and hurled my small body onto the bed and prepared myself for the possibility of meeting my great-great-grandfather sooner than I had expected.

I heard the door open quietly and looked over. Oh, good, I thought. She wasn't carrying a heated poker (paddle; switch; anything). Before she could say anything, I cried out, "MOM, YOU DON'T LOVE ME." To which she replied, "I do love you, and I'LL DO ANYTHING TO PROVE IT." She then picked up my filthy, muddy feet and kissed them. Needless to say, that experience taught me a great deal about the meaning of repentance and forgiveness. . . .

—Matthew S. Holland, "Muddy Feet and White Shirts"
General Conference, April, 1983.

The most important work you will ever do will be within the walls of YOUR OWN HOME.

—Harold B. Lee

Teach her to look to the Author and Finisher
of her faith for her validation and worth.
Help her to fear only God and not man.
And remind her that the mission-field
of home is a battleground worth fighting for.

—Kelly Crawford

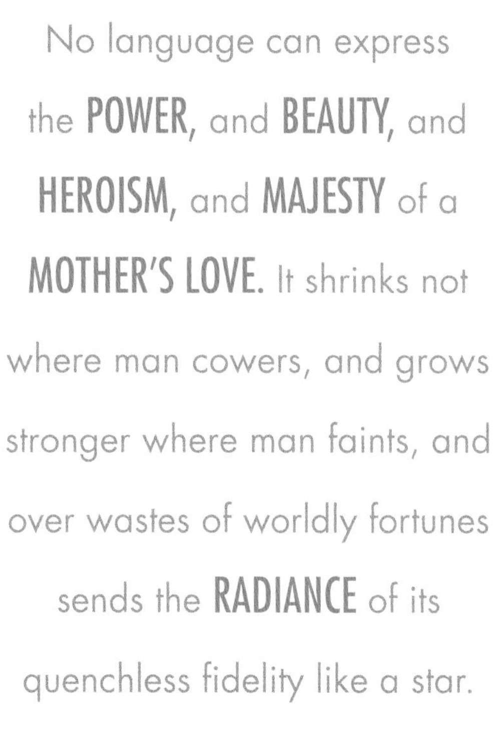

No language can express the **POWER**, and **BEAUTY**, and **HEROISM**, and **MAJESTY** of a **MOTHER'S LOVE.** It shrinks not where man cowers, and grows stronger where man faints, and over wastes of worldly fortunes sends the **RADIANCE** of its quenchless fidelity like a star.

—Edwin Hubbell Chapin

A MOTHER'S

HUG

LASTS LONG AFTER

AFTER SHE LETS GO.

FEW OF US WILL →
REACH OUR POTENTIAL
WITHOUT THE
nurturing
OF BOTH THE
MOTHER
WHO BORE US
→ AND THE ←
MOTHERS WHO BEAR
WITH US.

—Sheri L. Dew

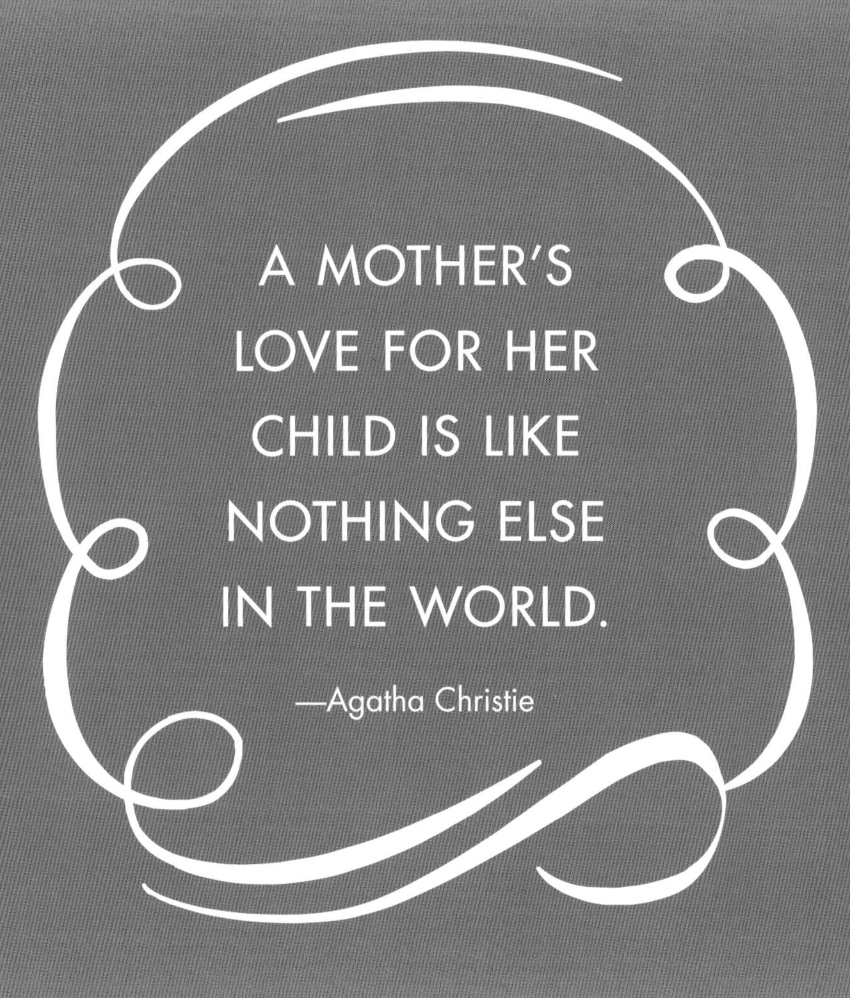
A MOTHER'S
LOVE FOR HER
CHILD IS LIKE
NOTHING ELSE
IN THE WORLD.
—Agatha Christie

CHILDREN:
they were
HIS
before they were
OURS.

I love these

LITTLE PEOPLE;

and it is not a slight thing when they, who are so fresh from God,

LOVE US.

—Charles Dickens

BEING A MOTHER IS NOT ABOUT WHAT YOU GAVE UP TO HAVE A CHILD, BUT WHAT YOU'VE GAINED FROM HAVING ONE.

—Sunny Gupta

THERE IS ETERNAL INFLUENCE AND POWER IN MOTHERHOOD.

—Julie B. Beck

ARE NOT THE ONES WHO HAVE NEVER STRUGGLED. THEY ARE THE ONES **WHO NEVER GIVE UP,** DESPITE THE STRUGGLES.

—SHARON JAYNES

Moms are like
buttons...
they hold
everything together.

MY DEAR SISTERS, YOUR HEAVENLY FATHER LOVES YOU—EACH OF YOU. THAT LOVE NEVER CHANGES. IT IS NOT INFLUENCED BY YOUR APPEARANCE, BY YOUR POSSESSIONS, OR BY THE AMOUNT OF MONEY YOU HAVE IN YOUR BANK ACCOUNT. IT IS NOT CHANGED BY YOUR TALENTS AND ABILITIES. IT IS SIMPLY THERE. IT IS THERE FOR YOU WHEN YOU ARE SAD OR HAPPY, DISCOURAGED OR HOPEFUL. GOD'S LOVE IS THERE FOR YOU WHETHER OR NOT YOU FEEL YOU DESERVE LOVE. IT IS SIMPLY ALWAYS THERE.

—THOMAS S. MONSON

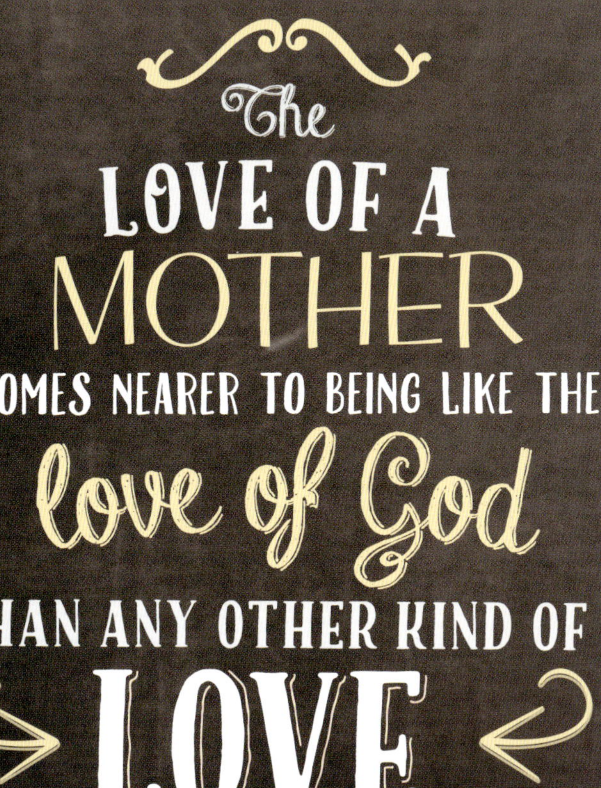
The
LOVE OF A
MOTHER
COMES NEARER TO BEING LIKE THE
love of God
THAN ANY OTHER KIND OF
LOVE.
—JOSEPH F. SMITH

Mom tried to give each of us some personal time with her. My needs were a little different from my sisters'. By the time I was twelve, my mom determined that she needed to give me more **ONE-ON-ONE TIME.** She began sitting by my bed at night before I fell asleep. I wasn't much into visiting, but Mom would still come and sit by me four or five times during the week. If she started to give advice or counsel, I would turn over and tell her that I loved her but good night. **SO OFTEN SHE SAT BY ME** without saying anything, just being a comforting presence. This went on throughout my teenage years.

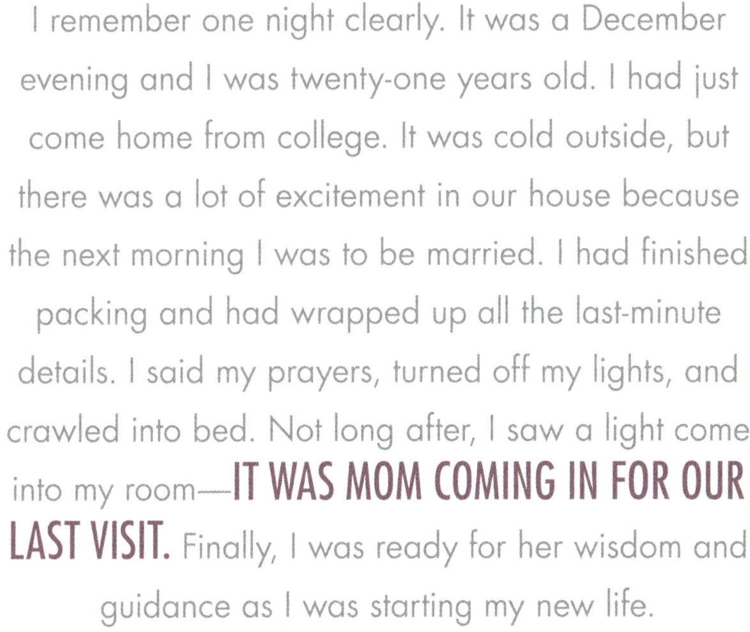

I remember one night clearly. It was a December evening and I was twenty-one years old. I had just come home from college. It was cold outside, but there was a lot of excitement in our house because the next morning I was to be married. I had finished packing and had wrapped up all the last-minute details. I said my prayers, turned off my lights, and crawled into bed. Not long after, I saw a light come into my room—**IT WAS MOM COMING IN FOR OUR LAST VISIT.** Finally, I was ready for her wisdom and guidance as I was starting my new life.

Jana Peterson Staples, "The Remarkable Vision of My Mother," *Mothers of Faith*, p. 18.

A MOTHER'S
♥ HEART ♥
IS ALWAYS
WITH HER
CHILDREN.

If a child
is not listening, don't despair.
Time and truth
are on your side. At the
right moment,
your words
will return as if from
heaven itself.
Your testimony will
never leave your children.

—Neil L. Andersen

Making the decision to have
a child—it is momentous.
It is to decide forever
to have your
HEART
go walking around
outside your body.

—Elizabeth Stone

NO GIFT TO YOUR MOTHER
CAN EVER EQUAL
HER GIFT TO YOU–LIFE.

–ANONYMOUS

Because I feel that, in the Heavens above,
The angels, whispering to one another,
Can find, among their burning terms of love,
NONE SO DEVOTIONAL AS THAT OF "MOTHER."

—Edgar Allan Poe

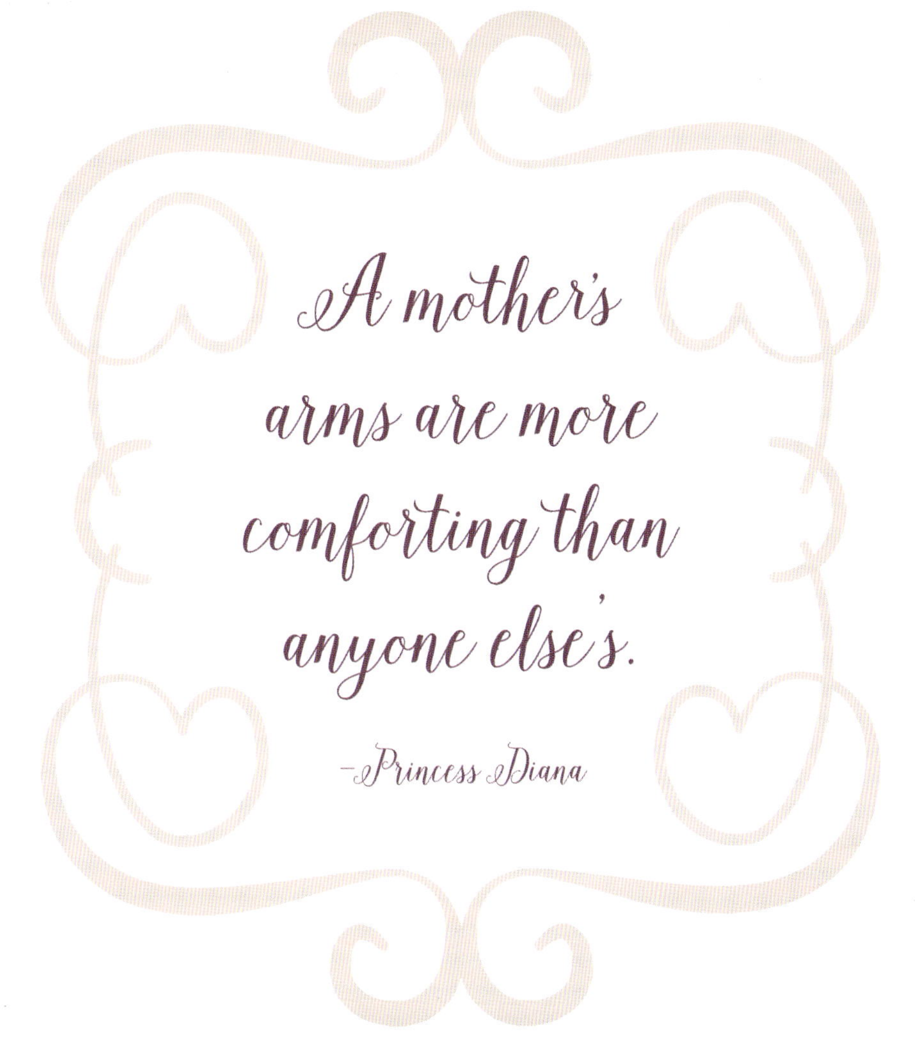
A mother's
arms are more
comforting than
anyone else's.
–Princess Diana

Cover and interior design by Christina Marcano

Published by Covenant Communications, Inc.
American Fork, Utah

Printed in China
First Printing: March 2016

22 21 20 19 18 17 16 10 9 8 7 6 5 4 3 2 1

ISBN-13: 978-1-68047-960-7